PETER OW
early years ir
working as a
ordained, becoming a parish priest in
1992. He has since written a handful
of books and presented several award-winning
television programmes. At the time of writing he
still serves as a parish priest in Sussex, England.

CONVERSATIONS WITH NATURE

Peter Owen Jones

Edited by Imogen Lycett Green

Illustrated by Jerry Shearing

CLAIRVIEW

Clairview Books Ltd.,
Russet, Sandy Lane,
West Hoathly,
W. Sussex RH19 4QQ

www.clairviewbooks.com

Published by Clairview Books 2022

A CIP catalogue record for this book is available from the
British Library

ISBN 978 1 912992 41 6

Cover by Morgan Creative
Typeset by Symbiosys Technologies, Visakhapatnam, India
Printed and bound by 4Edge Ltd, Essex

For Helen Merrilees

Contents

Foreword

These luminous words have the weight of much listening about them. Just a few sentences a day will fill us with protein. This is the domain of direct encounter: no arid philosophising but a great nose for what Dylan Thomas calls the 'green fuse' of everything.

Conversations with Nature has a surprise when you really start to attend to its disclosures. A high moral bar. To engage with the sandpiper and the bear, the storm and the seed means to work on the fundament of our character. Or to *get* worked on. It's inescapable. The book has an excavation of conscience at its centre. We remember something we once glimpsed. But not by receiving a scolding, but rather by a consistent announcement of the heart. It's an old secret that most of our soul lives outside of our body, and some rare dialogue is being witnessed here, a psyche seeking echo-location with the tawny owl and the field mouse. Peter bangs into the stuff of life and finds it tremendous.

1

Like the turning seasons he spares us not the wild flower meadow or the lightning storm; I find myself returning again and again to these words:

The house of peace is built from the flints of suffering.

And the embers of peace Peter blows upon are not some privately curated equilibrium, but a peace between every living thing. That's a mighty commitment to something radical in agency, a glimpse of Eden. That's a peace unlikely to be realised in one lifetime. We feel the years now gathered in Peter, and I love the earned weight of his experience – his sorrows and substantial joys – that are all so present here. Everything is invited to the table.

Many of us have dry mouths and this is succulent wine. I will carry this little book in my pocket with chocolate and a hip flask. I will read the words on London buses and in Dartmoor woods. These across-species conversations are more than reverie, they are *participation*.

W. B. Yeats once said, 'I'm looking for the face I had before the world was made.' Wonderful and typically mystical. Peter finds his face *in* the world; he locates sustenance in communion with turtle, foxglove and love-struck pilgrims hooting at the moon. Inside all of these things is a universe within a universe. He has gifted us something subtle and dynamic, much of which could be carved on a breastplate in the chaos of our times.

Martin Shaw

Prologue

Once we were dust, a single cell. Here, illuminated in the void. We travelled through many forms, through unknowing, through becoming, many deaths, many births, learning to feel, to respond. We travelled through water and out onto the land, we took our first breath as we all still do. It has taken billions of years for each one of us to reach here. To reach this splendour.

Over this time, which is no time, we learned to see ever outwards into clarity. Between the leaves, the lines of water light, into the grasslands, into the great white winters, into amber and carnelian, into paths and tides and stars. We were one form among many forms in the garden. We learned to hear the voices of the mountains, the rivers, the sky, of silence. The mice spoke, the trees spoke, the stars spoke, the deer and the fox spoke, the snake spoke, and from these words we made being. From these words came fire and paint, fields and memory, the past, the present and the future. From these words we made homes and kingdoms, weapons, mandalas. These words formed great cities and their machines ever clamouring, and we let the silence slip and the words of the whispering world fall away beyond the mirror of our making.

Peter Owen Jones

July 2022

The Khamsin Speaks of the Storm

You are born into an empty house. And slowly at first, seeping through the windows, come the words of days, the words of crows and gulls, the language of leaves. In time, faces appear, the faces of flowers, the face of the lion, of the deer, the faces of butterflies and fish. And you may dance with the lemurs and hide your very soul in the hills, in the seas, in the arms of the grove, but I will find you.

I will follow you into the roots of the oak and tear her down. Find you resting on the banks where the clear pools gleam and strike the lightning in. I will rip the nest from the tree. I will send in the sand to ruin your fields, to suffocate your wells of hope. Throw the raven onto your path. Turn the rain to grit and take the roof from the thickets and scatter your fawns for the wolves. I will bring the quarrelling sparrows into your night to haunt your towers in the land of stones.

I will be there to greet you as you walk away from the fresh earth on his grave. I am at the door as she betrays you, hands you the cup of foxgloves and nightshades. I will drive you out from your rooms and walls into ditches, into winter, into the wood of thorns and dress your wounds with the sap from the poppy until you beg to be cut again. Until you know this place as your own. Until you know the lion of revenge as yourself. That the constant rain of sorrow comes to sweep your house clean.

Watch the fires, see how I feed the kites and the crows, that when the oak falls I lay a bed for the light, for the willow herb, there is new grass for the fawns. How I carry seeds and the birds to new lands, fashion new pools for the shore, that the flood is feed for winter's fields.

And I will not be calmed by the innocence of spring, the swelling of summer. Even the rocks I will break into pieces, the earthquake will open the burrow, the fire drive you into the cave and there we will meet and speak of sorrow, of bears and crows, of love and the end of all things.

12

The Windflower Speaks of Flux

Yesterday is not a tomb. There is no wall between what is now and what was then and what is to come. It is one. A petal apart from the flower has no meaning.

There was rain. I closed my petals and rested. In the dream, the cloud moved on, the starlight returned and as the air warmed, there was a new song, new scents, a new breeze. Everything is moving. Now the ants through the stems, the brief wing of birds, leaves shaping shadows, the unseen sap ever flowing in the boughs. The gleaning bees, the heartbeat of night and day. Everything is moving.

Look into the mirror of the pond, the reflection changing with every ripple of wind. The moon moves the tides, the tides move the sand, not one of Mundaka's waves is like another. The thrush does not build the same nest, neither does the gull fly the same line. I cannot know the murmuration by counting the starlings. A flower opens when it will, the Pampero blows over the land, changing the colours of the hills. The warblers come and go as they choose. The moths and the bandicoots trawl the night. There is always arriving, there is always leaving, the turning of birth and death, the running of joy and sorrow, everything is moving.

You and I are born on the farthest shore that life has reached. We are sons and daughters of this unfolding, of this churning, of this revolving, this transforming. The egg becoming the song, the tree becomes the seed, the cliff is becoming sand, the rain is becoming the wave, grass becomes milk, it is ceaseless. This revelation. Do the rivers ever rest? Are the clouds ever still? The soil is seething. To say that the rose started here and ended there is of no consequence unless I received her becoming. I have this day, I have this breath, this dance with the grass, with the wind, with the red-crowned crane, with the star, with you.

The Fox Speaks of Exile

At night, after the evening mists have settled,
I rise, and like you I enter a land I do not know,
neither does it know me. We are adrift, not knowing but feeling. In the day, wandering in the starlight, down all those stone streets and sparkling
paths. Does the desert know the forest? The fish
know the field? The baobab know the white
wastes of Svalbard? No, we are marooned, our
blood merely borrowed from the earth, our eyes
and feet the edges of an island that no more knows
the sea it lies within, than the jasmine knows the
sap running through the stem. Need, desire, hunger, they are an inheritance, they do not belong to
you and me. What we share with every tree, every
wolf, even the mice there in the land of stones is
the great gift of not knowing.

I can fool myself with illusions of belonging. That
I know this way through the night, it is the path
my father walked and I have my mother's stories
about beginning and ending and how the moon
gave birth to the first vixen. And I can dance with

their bones through the seasons round the night fire, but when morning comes, I stand alone, a stranger to the trees, to the birds, to the air. Look at the sky forever travelling, the river in an endless searching, you and I believing that in the distance, beyond the hills, beyond the sea lies the feast, the garden, the wedding, the word.

I can follow the paths through the field of flowers and on into the distance where they say at its end the angels will meet me and make flutes from my bones. I can follow her as she leads me into the garden and feeds me milk and seeds, but love makes an orphan of us all. And at night, heavy with dew, I speak to the stars; they seem in their stillness to be knowing the self-same exile. 'It is from here you begin,' they say.

The Mayfly Speaks of Impermanence

You have no claim on the next heartbeat, your heartbeat does not belong to you. Your heartbeat comes from the beginning of feeling, the beginning of knowing, passed down from the fish to the bird, through the lemur's hands. From the gazelle to the lion, from the marram grass to the banyan to the kestrel's nest. In every egg, inside every seed is folded the skin of the drum. In the seed of the hare, in the seed of the woman, in the seed of the darkling beetle leaning on the Namib sand to gather the mist. Your heartbeat is a gift, from one life to the next. You share it with the wren, with the ox, with the whale. I share my heartbeat with yours.

Your heartbeat is the ticket to the dance, to the swarm, to the weeping, to the fear. It is your guarantee of uncertainty, it will pursue you to the end. To the end of breathing, the end of loving, the end of breaking, the end of believing. You can retreat to the trench at the side of the road, take the upward steps to the towers of knowledge or follow them as they lead down into the earth where, in time, your torch will fail. And when you return from the places of forgetting, from the garden, from the land of stones, the truth weighs heavier still.

There is nothing here that belongs to you. The stones are not yours, the river is not yours, the winter, the spring are not yours. Not even your skin, not even your death belongs to you. Your dying is every dying. You can be pain, you can be fear, you can be hunger. You can be the dance, be the silence, be the morning, you can be the space. The wren is not singing, the wren is the song.

Everything exists between everything else. Between the tree and its reflection, between the jasmine and the bear. Between the flower and the fish, between the star and the moon. Why then would you even consider that life belongs to you? The harder you hold on to it, the more fragile it becomes. It is the fragile door that opens into beauty.

The Mouse Speaks of Courage

When the wind blows the gate open, when the gulls call your name, it is time.

The journey through the field of flowers is yours to make. The journey waits for you, you do not wait for the journey. You may prepare through many lifetimes to make it, and you will know when you are ready. You will begin to feel becalmed, the years, the days turned into the pattern of your making. When the mastering of the hour is no more than a preparation for the next one. When you sense you have become a prisoner in the very house you have laboured to construct. When you finally wear the crown, then you will hear the crying of the wrens and the taunting of the crows. Then the wind will be at your door, your window to claim her wandering seed planted in every womb, and sing your name from the farthest horizon. It is the song that calls the smolt to the sea, the shoot from the seed, the eagle to the sky, the fawn to stand. The song to draw you from the satisfaction of your answers, your tables and grain. There is no need to announce your leaving. Take only what you can carry, nothing more. Open the door and enter the field of flowers. Wear the crowns. Stitch them from the grass and daisies waiting.

You are the beloved, the princeling. The queen of all the green ground. The clear-faced petals wait upon your gaze, the buds upon your birth, the daffodil maidens waving, lavender serving scent and balm. Now you remember skipping, and how it feels to hold a hand as small as yours. To walk alone through the great rhododendron halls, the world of rushes, to look into the gaze of the rose and enter the dusk of thickets. To lie down in the meadow's gown. Here there is honey, fruit and corn. But yours is not the only need, yours are not the only teeth.

The cats wait, they are the colour of night and leaves and there is always the wolf, the leopard, the snake, the peril of cuts and ice. You share hunger with the lynx, the vulture, in this field you are prey, your flesh for their life. You are bark and water and earth, you are no different from every prince, from every queen in every form. When the teeth strike, when the poison spreads, you meet them alone. Nowhere in the field of flowers is safe. This is a fragile place; here, you are fragile.

To cross this field you will need to unearth your compass long buried. Buried under stone, buried under layers of ideas and assumptions, buried beneath beliefs and maps and learning, beneath shame. To find it, stand alone and let the darkness thicken and surround you. Meet the fear, let it hold you, let it swarm. Know that it is necessary to be fragile, to be afraid, fear is merely the warning bell, do not hate it, feel it, but do not make fear your guide, know it and let it pass. Now the compass will turn within you. Touch the distance. Here are the eyes that see through the dark, the ears that hear the silent owls, now you can smell water and taste the honey. And in the morning when you rise, walk with your palms open and the deer will be your companion, the sparrows will bring you fruit and grain and the wolf will walk by your side. It is not might that leads you through the field of flowers. It is reverence. It is love.

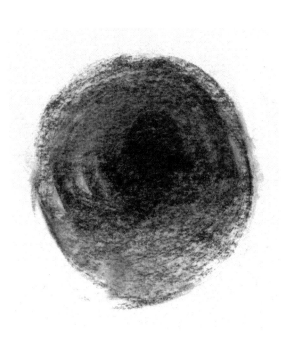

The Olm speaks of Khthonios

Walk into the cave. Walk beyond the light, until in every direction there is nothing other than complete darkness. Here you are beyond the sky, beyond the heron, beyond even the land of stones, beyond blood and bone. Place your hands in the water and I will meet you. I will show you the wounded man, the wounded woman, the kennel of the dog, the cellars that hold the pike, the bear in chains, the crypt full of thorns where the shrike hangs the robins.

There is nothing to be said. Not until you remove your mask. The mask of the dove, the mask of the bull, the mask of the mouse. Only then will you see clearly. The lost child, the swarms of your fear, how you lay within the folds of the nest whilst all the while assembling revenge. The wrens you snared, the fawns you betrayed, the fields you poisoned with lies. The knife you carry to cut the horses and the wings off swallows, to cut the earth.

And I will place in your hands uncovered the knotted threads of all you hold unforgiven, run them through your fingers until they become your prayer. I will place in your palms the stones of revenge, grind them together until they are grains for the soil. In this darkness, the wolves are behind you, you will hear their breathing until you embrace the void. In here the water runs with weeping until you know it as your own.

As the tender stem.

As the broken wing.

As the loving moss.

As the homeless son.

The Bear Speaks of Carnage

I am here to desolate your house, to kill your brothers, your fathers, your mothers and their children. In every season I am set against you, your hunger against mine, your will against mine, your courage is measured by my courage. Yet, we are both innocent. Face me, as the roach will face the pike, as the hare will face the wolf, as the bee faces the hornet, the tree, the storm. What minnow, what sparrow, what lion, what deer ever died of old age? It is shaming to die of old age and worse to tremble with mourning. Does the sea grieve for the spent waves, the soil break its silence for the flower's end? You can lay your tables, build your palaces, cover the ground in stone, but all the while I am waiting. The dogs are waiting, even the mice held up in the barns are waiting to lay your house to waste, every chamber, every store, every nursery until it is utterly silent. Until the wind in time brings it down, until it fades into the place of forgetting.

Then all that lies in the earth, the remnant packs, the sons of ivy curled, will rise. The mice will rise, the dogs, the deer, the sandpiper will rise and I will walk imperious through the newly born forests and for one day, dance with the deer and the dogs. When tomorrow comes, I will tend my thirst and kill again.

The Robin Speaks of Death

I am by your side. In the dance, in the sunshine towns, in the land of stones. I hear you when you fall, as you breathe, as the river rises around you. And I am with you on the hill, as you feast on the horizon, as you are drawn to the edges of the seas. Look at the wave, it breaks on the shore and will arrive in time on another, it is ceaseless. Life holds death, death holds life.

Lay down, my love. Lay down your scrape of earth, the dance, the grip of rain on hours and days; every blade of grass and heavy stone; the burrows where you keep your crows, hide your thorns and wings; the cave where you store her face, his hands.

Today is not in one place and tomorrow in another, the butterfly and the hare are not divided, the grass and the air are not divided, earth is in heaven, heaven is in earth. Existence is not bound in feathers, in fins. You were never entombed in flesh, neither is the earth your resting place. There are many earths, many heavens, there are many times.

And time may rule the bone and the feather, the leaf and the skin. But time has no call on the singing and on the song, time has no call on to whom you give your heart, and where the hare makes her bed, has no tenure over hope, over dreaming, over even the beginning and the end.

This is the work of love.

Lay down, my love, lay down, open your hand, you are not marooned. I am waiting, I am on the other side of the hill. Here. Every spoken word of love is held, is alive, remains.

The Heron Speaks of Sadness

There will be many days when the cloud is down, when it is not possible to dance, they say. There are two hundred days of winter beyond death, one thousand days of winter beyond betrayal. I will meet you on the edge of the grey lake, come alone. I will wait for you in the land of stones. I will follow you as you venture into the winter woods, into the half-light over the scattered bones on the lifeless ground beneath the close-planted pines. Once you have entered this world, you will be here without spring, without summer for as long as you are content to be rescued from it.

You may wander for weeks, for months, some wander for years, it is true to say that some never return. They stumble deeper into the half-light and in time, lose all sight of beauty. Here they become quickly old, they become wounded. Sadness is the infection in the wound, it is the wounding of beauty. But even here at the far reaches of the land of stones, at the edge of life, I am waiting.

Show me the heavy seeds you have carried this far, the stream where all the fishes lay poisoned on the bank, the nest in the hay where the kittens were slaughtered. The wasteland of the wheat fields, the afternoon darkness under raining skies, the cold days of summer, the face of your betrayer. When you hear the autumn wind sobbing for her children, the blind flower crying, then sadness has found a way in. Sadness is not mourning, mourning has its season. Sadness breaks in through the wound, through a broken door into the garden, and plants a bitter seed that is carried from one generation to the next. It is the work of sorrow to gather these seeds.

When you see me flying alone in the evening sky, look at me, I am laden down carrying the bitter seeds of sadness that I have been given. At night I will leave them on a shore and the tides and the storm will take them and lay them down in the graves of the sea.

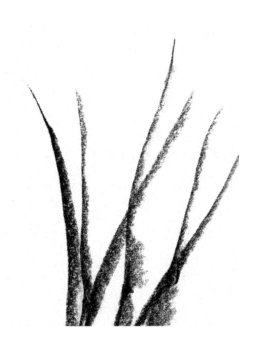

44

The Daisy Speaks of Receiving

Everything is given. The rain, the seed, the light from the star, the grape, the storm. You exist through receiving. The sheep receives the grass, the grass receives the rain, the albatross receives the air, have you seen the way water receives light? Each breath you take is a receiving. The apple receives the soil, the starling receives the apple, the earth receives the seeds. To be fully receptive is to be completely open, as the flower is open to receive the starlight, the bee. To be partially receptive means you only partially receive. You only ever have half of what you really need. Half of love, half of the storm, half of the revelation. To receive in full means to experience fully what is being given. The sweetness of grace, the purity of sorrow, the gaze returned, the voice of intuition. To receive is to be vulnerable, to know yourself as the beggar, the orphan, the fawn, stranded, set out to be lost. Your bearings are your walls, how can you receive the new morning if you are carrying, weighed down with pieces of yesterday? How are you to befriend the deep silence of the night unless you learn how to receive the fear that guards it?

You have received your body, every cell of skin, every strand of hair is beautifully made. Your eyes, your fingers, your heart is beautifully made. Receive, if you can, the wounds of love, it is not your heart that breaks it is merely the wall around it, and beyond the wall receive the garden. Receive the wolf as you receive the fawn, this is one of the many measures of love.

The Turtle Speaks of Communion

Knowledge hardens in time. Sets as a shell.

I assumed the work of life was to live, to survive, to learn. I learned the colours of water, how to read the shadows of the sailfish and the sharks. Learned the language of the shoals, of the shallows, the pathways through the cold kelp seas, and how the starlight catches the grim nets of man. I always loved the gatherings in the gardens of the reefs, and the laying nights out beyond the waves into the sand, the feeling of release. Another cycle completes, and the sense of emptiness beyond it. But as I said, knowledge hardens in time and what is new turns old. It is a contraction, a shrinking, a waning of colour, the enduring of days and grain by grain and wave by wave the shell hardens, the mystery flattens and what remains is the motion of eating, the motion of sleeping, the necessity of speaking.

After ninety-three years, I stopped counting. Is a life measured in time? Am I to know the waves by their height and their number, the moray by length, the rain in inches? So I resolved to forget, to forget hunger, to forget desire, to forget believing. And farther and deeper I dived to the darkness, into the emptiness, into the absolute stillness. I had heard her name, that she had been seen close by Sangalaki, Derawan and Spa Island, that she was waiting just beyond the break. Her presence was always felt. Then one day down in the deep I heard her voice.

'Come,' she said

'Where are we going?', I asked.

'I do not know,' she replied. I knew she was Themis.

Her shell was a garden of many different seaweeds, barnacles and anemones living around the rim. She had a train of small fishes and seahorses that attended her. And in the shallows and the azure blue of the white sand bays, others would join – triggerfish, hawkfish, angelfish, groupers, snappers and great crowds of yellow-tailed damsels. It was a procession, just to be in her presence. At night sometimes we rested on the surface between the worlds. We journeyed through oceans, to the shallows, to the gardens, the inner reefs.

She never spoke until one day she said quietly: 'Receive the current. Let the current lead you. It is the hardest thing. It is the easiest thing.'

She would always attend the laying. Waiting just before the break, and would return for the hatching and watch as the frigates and vultures devoured the young. It was early one morning, the sea was still and we rose to watch the hatching on Messinia, it was dark and yet I could see vague shapes appearing on the sand. It was man. And in the dawn I watched as men and women sat down. They crossed their legs, they closed their eyes, they did not speak. As the sun rose, the hatchlings ran between them, not knowing that they were even there. The frigates and the vultures did not come down, and thousands reached the sea.

The Jasmine Flower Speaks
of Enchantment

Come, my love. Within my leaves to where my petals lie, to this table laid with hay and honey, to the seat of feasting and forgetting. Dance with me step by step around the fire until we stand between time and eternity, between female and male, between the butterfly and the bird, until we are weightless.

Undress. Leave your clothes and your compass at the door. I am waiting for you there on the wide ledges leading out from the Sinai caves as the dawn is cast in lilac and amber, where the martins leave their beds and take to the air as one. The rose is waiting for you to arrive, the moon and the south wind, they sing your name continually. Come, taste the scent of the earth as the rain falls on the Rub' al Khali, the mist embracing the autumn trees in the valleys of England.

As a child, you followed me into the summer barn, we lay down in a shaft of light and I danced in the glittering dust. We walked hand in hand into the garden, where the blossoming apple tree spreads his branches over the morning water, where the Muscovy and the fox sit together, where the rushes and the sky are one.

You will know me because I give milk and light and ask for nothing in return. But you must also know the snake will dance before she strikes, the path leading into the deep shadows of sorrow is scented with the nectar of the sundew. That the fruit of the brightly petalled poppies will sing you to the dying stars.

You do not have to carry with you the earth on your grave. I am by your side always, let us walk together through the light on the water, let us take off our shoes and leave our footprints in the cool sand under the beach-blown junipers on the southern shores of Crete. When evening falls, we will light the Palo Santo, burn some sage and like the river and the earth, the oak and the air, fall asleep embracing. You are my love, you are my love.

The Hawthorn Speaks of Aphrodisia

I see you. Your hands within the ferns. Your hair within the horse's mane, your hips rising in the rivers seething. You lie naked over the southern hills and break the meadow's bread. Your scent is bound thick in the evening woods, in the yeasting leaves, the mushroom gills, there in the mud and the moss.

I am the mares calling the stallions in, the drifting pollen, the swollen stamen.

I am the seed impregnating the soil. The rain impregnating the earth.

I am the jasmine impregnating the night, the star impregnating the morning. You can call this love. The making of hands and wings, the fermenting of tigers and shrews. But do not call it shame, not the wielding of lips, the secrets of scent and the patience of eggs.

I am awake for you always, I will look for you always, on every path, on every horizon, in every moon.

And I will wait for you, in the mud and moss, in the yeasting leaves. I will wait a thousand years and kill bears, and cover my skin in clay and ash and dance your breath with stags and storks and beg for your flood, your scent and sweat to drown in.

And when we meet, we will lock the gates. We will bend like stems and fold a nest from night and call like bulls and birds. And writhe in the spate that made the dogs, the lions, the rioting flies and be the wild horses breathing, the hyacinth rising.

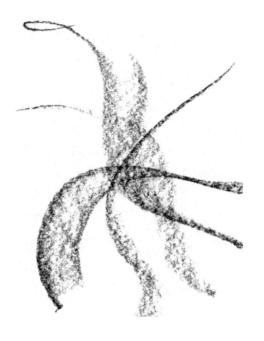

60

The Painted Lady Speaks of Reverie

I slept for nine days without waking, there in the leaf world.

I woke with wings paved rose pink and layered with cinnamon and white sphurana. I heard the river laughing, the marigolds in full mirth and ran through the land of brides, the orchard almond towns. Faster, and higher, around Toubkal and Ouanoukrim and through miles of silent stones then palms, and out over the white waves.

And on, over your stern towers, the sobbing of your sirens, a merciless grid of fields. Why do you furrow your brow with gates and walls? You are woken with singing. Have you not seen the morning greetings? How the desert opens the day? That there is joy when the river meets the sea, an embracing? That the seedling is joy, the orchid is joy, the suckling foals, the seals in the swell, the ravens playing? How even the ivy shines?

While you fill your days with counting and carrying, the magpies are merrying, otters are spinning stones, the pomegranate is flowering, ripples are weaving lagoons and the mountain streams are gambolling down. Why are you cast inside as the gate of the night opens, when the petunia flowers and the moths are giddy with mead?

I was born in Eden and will arrive in Jannah. There for the wedding of the meadow and the seed, the path and the moon, the river and the star. And I will whirl for the pauper, for the meek, over the battleground and within the prison walls. I will skip through the potter's field. Even as the lines on my wings deepen, the colours slip, I will not cease. Neither will the waters give up their love of light, nor the buttercup relent. Come, we will drink with the rooks, feast in the buddleia halls and roll with the morpho and the stoats unbound.

The Starling Speaks of Dancing

From the breath, came the formless void. From the void came the breath and from the breath came the breeze.

The breeze danced into a wind and the wind danced over the deep. Danced cold into warmth and the warmth into a flame and the flame into fire.

And the wind danced with fire and made stars and ash, and the ash danced with the air and made dust and the dust danced into clouds and earth.

The clouds danced with the earth and made skies and rain, and the rain danced into rivers and seas.

And the rivers danced with the earth and made grass, and the grass danced into oaks into baobabs, into jasmine and ferns.

The jasmine danced with the moon and made tides, and the tides danced with the star and made fishes and shells, the great whites and the moving shoals.

And the fish danced with the shore and made dragons and lizards, and the lizards danced into leopards, into mice and lions, into horses and red-crowned cranes, into starlings.

And the starling danced into the murmuration.

And I will dance with my lovers, my sisters, my brothers, dance with the Khamsin, dance with the heron, dance with the day. Dance with the dusk because there is no price on dancing. And should there be a time when the starlings are gone, then the sparrows will dance in their place. And when the sparrows are no more, the flies will take the dancing on, the leaves will take the dancing on, the deserts and the meadows will take the dancing on. The stones will take the dancing on.

The Oak Speaks of Sanctuary

The giving of sanctuary is written into the code of life. Planet earth is a sanctuary, a lifeworld in the midst of space. The stone gives sanctuary to the moss, the soil gives sanctuary to the seed, the river gives sanctuary to the reed, silence gives sanctuary to sound. You share this sanctuary with all life, with every grove, with every reef, with every moor and breath. A human being is called consciously to uphold and nurture the reality of sanctuary, to make it known, to bring it to life.

I will wait for you in the dance of leaves, there in the shadows among the light on the path, this is a door. I cannot offer you certainty, because there is none. I can celebrate the warmth of the air of each breath as it leaves my body, this is intimacy. I can tell you that there in the midst of the storm stands a tree and that at the base of the trunk is an opening within the roots just wide enough for you to enter. And within, there is a soft earth floor, the scent of pine, in here you are warm and dry. To find the tree, enter the storm.

The crows that arrive at my window, the bears at my door, they have not come to harm me, they have come to show me the way, to lead me to sanctuary. It is important for me to understand that I summoned them, they are not here of their own volition. They heard my loudening heartbeat, followed the scent of tears, watched as heartbreak broke me, saw me lost, drawing ever closer to the edge of life farther and farther out into the land of stones where the voices of the ones I love grow fainter and fainter. I am here at the edge of life to learn to build a shelter, that is what the stones are for. To build a strong tower, a stairway leading up to the one room with the bed and the blue sky window just above it. Glass doors open onto a terrace with flowers, the crows have become swallows and wolves dancers on the streets below.

I will not find sanctuary in love. I may find a shelter in the arms of the one I love, but this is not sanctuary, this is a place of prayer, it is the active state of communion. I cannot expect sanctuary in the realms of another's heart. Sanctuary is within, find the room within.

The Moss Speaks of Intimacy

Intimacy is the vessel, the first language of every lifeworld. It is intimacy that holds life in being, your life, my life. Every stem, every seed, every fin, every hair, every song. Intimacy is the child of devotion. The land embraces the lake. The soil is devoted to the seed. The sapling devoted to the star, the moss devoted to rain. The sea embraces the urchin, the shark, the glistening fish. The sand embraces the dead and broken shells. This is communion.

The cells of my body are intimate with each other, as are yours. The leaf is intimate with the root, the moon is intimate with the tide, your heart is intimate with your hands. Look at how close the blackbird must be to the night to begin the morning song.

Intimacy is the first calling you feel, calling you to suckle, to stand, to walk over the hill, to draw you into the light, to hear the leaves praising the rain, the waves praising the shore. I cannot know the rose by reason, the Gobi by marking her stones, the barley by weight. Without intimacy I am alone to this earth, I deny the bark, deny the rocks, deny the very rain and the dunnocks their nest. Look at how the rose opens completely. When you withhold your heart it withers. Then you are blind to the sorrow of the sickening fields, the darkening of the woods, you have chosen the land of stones.

Come, lie down on my bed made in the quiet canyons, 1 have laid a rug on the banks in the summering woods and there in the folds of Cadair Idris and Son Shan. Bring your wounds and the scars that lie hidden in your earth. Let the ferns hold you, the vines enter your skin, until you hear the bees praising the daisies and the rivers praising the reeds, the night stars praising your name. And when in time your heart breaks open, you will feel the jackdaws and the trees speaking, you will feel the depth of moss, the chalice of rain and know the Muscovy and the fox as yourself and the jewel you have become.

The Pond Speaks of Peace

Peace is boundless, without frontiers.

Before fire, before expansion, before dust and the heaving of worlds, the gatherings of form, all this is born from peace. Peace is the mother of this earth, the mother of every stem and star. Nurturing peace is the life purpose on all thriving planets. The greatest hope for human being is that one day you will choose to nurture peace, to know yourself on that surface, within those depths, to know what is found, that it is peace that holds a lifeworld in being, it is, above all things, the foremost reality.

The first reconciliation is between life and hunger. Life and hunger are tied. Hunger churns, continually stirs, it is ceaseless. Look at the wind always turning, the bears swaying through the Acadian forests in a constant waking search for food. Do the ants in their cities ever sleep? Are the tides ever still? Do the sparrows ever rest from their arguing? This hunger is the longing for existence. It is also the warm reach of death, calling.

The house of peace sits between the two, loving both aspects of itself.

The second reconciliation is with all other forms of life. I cannot know peace unless I am living in peace with every tree, with every bird, with every cloud, with the deer, with the snake and the nettle, with the very air itself. As long as one butterfly dies so that I may eat bread, my house is at war. When I harm the snail, I harm the thrush. When I harm the elver, I harm the heron. As I wound, so am I wounded. There can be no peace in a wounded house, only the cries for healing.

It is not possible to forge peace with a weapon. It is not possible to sustain peace with a weapon, those who keep weapons are the keepers of war. There can be no peace as long as the warrior is honoured above the child, above the householder, above the sparrow. Is the dragonfly greater than the swallow, are the willows greater than the water lilies, the baobab greater than the daisy? Not one is more deserving of honour than another.

The third reconciliation that you are being called to make is the reconciliation of the cross, the reconciliation between the priest and the warrior.

The house of peace is built from the flints of suffering. The grove is grown from the fruit of bitter seeds. Follow the path of your searching until you can read it no more, until you find yourself in the company of the flower, of the wolf and the deer. Follow the threads of love until they meet with peace.

Sit with me, see how the light and the water are one. That even in storms, the fierce hunger of desire, these pools are wells of calm. The depth of peace is found in stillness. You do not make peace, it is peace that makes you. And when it is your turn to leave this lifeworld, leave nothing broken behind.

Glossary

Arcadian forest. A temperate broad-leaved mixed forest in North America.

Bandicoot. A small marsupial native to Australia and New Guinea.

Baobab. A tree that grows in Africa, Australia and the Middle East.

Cadair Idris. A mountain in Wales.

Derawan. A turtle bay.

Elver. A young eel.

Hyacinth. A bulbous plant of the lily family with fragrant flowers.

Jannah. A paradise garden, the final abode of the righteous.

Khamsin. A hot southerly Egyptian wind.

Kelp. A large brown seaweed.

Kthonios. Beneath the earth, subterranean.

Marram grass. A grass that grows in sand dunes.

Messinia. A turtle beach.

Morpho. A South American species of butterfly.

Murmuration. A group of birds flying and moving as one.

Mundaka. A bay on the Atlantic coast of Spain.

Palo Santo. 'Sacred stick' in Spanish which burns with perfume.

Pampero. A South American wind.

Olm. A blind albino cave-dwelling salamander.

Ouanoukrim. A mountain in Morocco.

Rub al Khali. The empty desert of the Arabian peninsula.

Sangalaki. A turtle bay.

Son Shan. A sacred mountain in China.

Sphurana. A Sanskrit word meaning glittering, trembling, the sun upon the water.

Svalbard. A group of islands in the Greenland Sea.

Themis. A benevolent sea Goddess.

Toubkal. The highest peak in the Atlas mountains of Morocco.